Contents

Before you begin

Here is a list of some of the terms we use when explaining how to do each project. Before you start setting and looping, you must keep these things in mind.

C-clip: A c-clip as its name suggests, is a small, clear clip shaped like a "c" that we use to hold rubber bands together. C-clips are often the last step in a project. Some rubber band kits come with s-clips. Instead; you can use those the same way you use c-clips.

Hook: The hook is the off-white, hook-shaped utensil that is provided in the packaging of your loom. This is used to move rubber bands from their pegs instead of your fingers.

Threading: To thread beads onto your project wrap a thin piece of wire - such as a stripped twist tie around a single band. Add the beads onto the wire from the other end and then slide them onto the band.

Set up your loom square: When all of the columns are evenly set on the loom; no column of pegs is set forward or backward.

Offset: When columns in the loom are not square. For example when the outside columns are set evenly and the middle column is set one peg closer to you.

Getting started

Just like the looms, there are lots of types of bands and clips to choose from.

We show a C-shaped clip to join the bracelets, but you may have another shape; either will work. You could even use ribbon, cord or embroidery floss in place of the clip to dress up your creations.

Each project in this book will have a Chart to show where to place the bands, as well as illustrations to show looping the bands.

To the right is a blank Chart like the ones that will show band placement. Each ∪ shape represents a loom pin.

The band's colour & direction will be shown on the Chart & illustrations. It's very important to follow the Steps when placing & looping the bands on the loom pins.

On the illustrations, the band that you are working with is shown in colour. Bands that are in the background or not being used for that Step are shown in a much lighter colour.

Let's get started with a basic Single Bracelet in red & aqua where you'll learn to place & loop the bands.

PIN

SINGLE

LEVEL: Easy-Peasy

NOTE: When placing the bands: • Place the loom on the table with the open parts of the pins facing away from you. • This bracelet only uses 2 rows of pins.

Step 1

Use your fingers to place a red band on the loom Push it down on the pins.

Step 2

Then add an aqua band & push it down on the pins.

Step 3

Continue to place red & aqua bands on the loom pins until you reach the top of the loom (see the chart of the left).

Step 1

Use the looping tool to go down into the centre pin hole. Move the red band out of the way & grab the aqua band with the hook. Pull it up & off the pin.

Step 2

Keeping the band on the hook, loop the aqua band over the pin to the left; remove the hook.

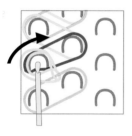

Step 3

Go down into the next pin hole on the left & pick up the red band.
Pull it up & off the pin.

Step 4

Loop the red band over
to the centre pin

Step 5

Continue picking up & looping the red and aqua bands until you've looped the last red band.

Step 6

Slide a C-clip over the red band loops.

Step 7

Carefully pull all the bands from the pins.

Step 8

Join the bracelet by slipping the C-clip through the loop at the beginning of the bracelet.

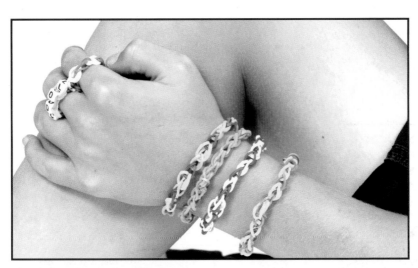

THAT'S IT, YOU'VE DONE IT!

Well done you have just made your first loom band bracelet. Try making these in different colours to practice working with the loom & looping tool. You can also make a matching ring using 9-10 bands.

TRIPLE SINGLE
LEVEL: Easy-Peasy

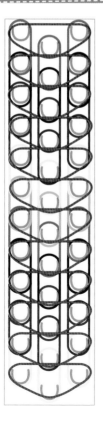

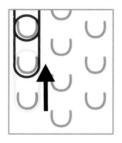

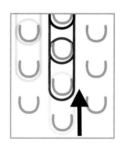

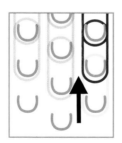

Step 1-3

Place bands on each pin row, starting with yellow & referring to the chart on the left for colour sequence.

Step 4

Place white bands (shown in grey) in triangles (see the Chart on the left)

Step 1

Grab the blue band
on the left pin

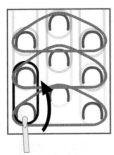

Step 2

Loop the blue band
straight up to the next pin

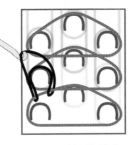

Step 3

Grab the blue band
on the centre pin

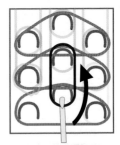

Step 4

Loop the blue band
straight up to the next pin

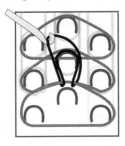

Step 5

Grab the blue band
on the right pin

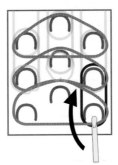

Step 6

Loop the blue band
straight up to the next pin

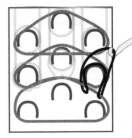

Step 7

Continue picking up & looping the bands until you reach
the top of the loom. Finish the bracelet with a white
extension & C-clip (see pages 33-34)

10

FISHTAIL

LEVEL: Medium

NOTE: When placing the bands:
• Place the loom on the table with the open parts of the pins facing left • Use your fingers to place the bands on the loom
• Follow the steps when placing the bands • Push each band down after you place it on the pins.

Step 1

Twist a yellow band into a figure 8 & place it on the pins

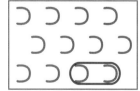
Step 2

Place the pink band on top of the yellow band

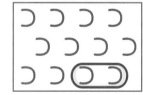
Step 3

Place a red band on top of the pink band

Step 1

Grab the yellow band on the left pin

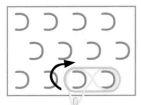

Step 2

Loop the band to the centre over the pink & red bands

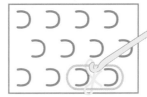

Step 3

Grab the yellow band on the right pin

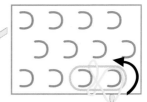

Step 4

Loop the band to the centre over the pink & red bands

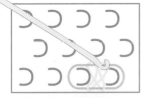

Step 5

Place a purple band on the pins

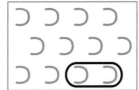

Step 6

Loop the pink band to the centre

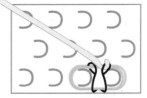

Step 7

Place a blue band on the pins

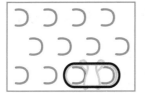

Step 8

Continue looping the bottom band to the centre

Step 8

Continue looping the bottom band to the centre & placing a new band on the pins. The bracelet will extend between the 2 pins

Step 9

When the bracelet is long enough, loop the bottom band to centre.

Step 10

Grab the last band from the pins & slide it on the looping tool

Step 11

Slide a C-clip on the band loops at the beginning & end to join

COLOUR IDEAS

Try other colour combinations. For two colours, alternate the colours on the pins & to make three colours, just repeat the colour sequence.

13

DIAMOND
LEVEL: Medium

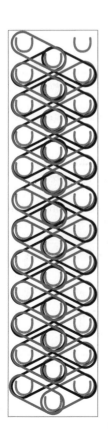

Step 1

Place the
first aqua band

Step 2

Place the
second aqua band

Step 3

Place the first
blue band

Step 4

Place the second
blue band

Step 5

Ending with 1 aqua band
at the top, continue to
place the aqua & blue
bands on the loom pins
until you reach the top of
the loom (see the chart
on page 14)

NOTE: When Looping the bands:
- Turn the loom around so the open parts of the pins are facing you
- Always use the looping tool to pick up & loop the bands

Step 1

Grab the top blue band
on the centre pin

Step 2

Loop the blue band
to the left pin

Step 3

Grab the remaining blue
band on the centre pin

Step 4

Loop the blue band to the right pin

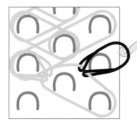

Step 5

Grab the aqua band on the left pin

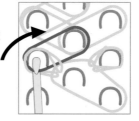

Step 6

Loop the aqua band to the centre pin

Step 7

Grab the aqua band on the right pin

Step 8

Loop the aqua band to the centre pin

Step 9

Continue picking up & looping the aqua & blue bands until you've looped the last set of bands.

Step 10

Refer to Steps 5-9 on page 33 to pull a new aqua loop through the center pin loops & to remove the bracelet from the loom. To finish the bracelet, refer to Step 5, page 34, to join the ends with a C-clip.

DOUBLE RHOMBUS
LEVEL: Medium

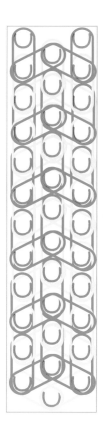

Step 1

Place the
first yellow band

Step 2

Place the
second yellow band

Step 3

Place the first green band

Step 4

Place the second green band

Step 5

Place the third green band

Step 6

Place the fourth green band

Step 7

Place the fifth green band

Step 8

Beginning with yellow, repeat from Step 3 to continue placing green & yellow bands on the loom pins until you reach the top of the loom (see the Chart on page 17). The last set of bands will only have four yellow bands.

Step 1

Grab the green band on the centre pin

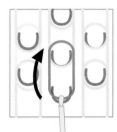

Step 2

Loop the green band straight up to the next pin

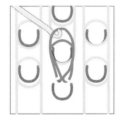

Step 3

Grab the green band on the left pin

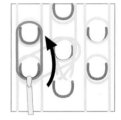

Step 4

Loop the green band straight up to the next pin

Step 5

Grab the green band on the right pin

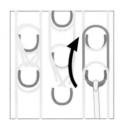

Step 6

Loop the green band straight up to the next pin

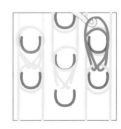

Step 7

Grab the top green band on the centre bin

Step 8

Loop the green band to the left to the next pin

Step 9

Grab the remaining green band on the centre pin

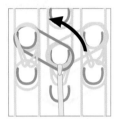
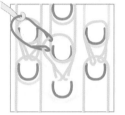
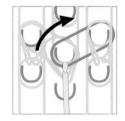

Step 10

Loop the green band to the right to the next pin

Step 11

Continue picking up & looping the yellow & green bands until you reach the last two yellow bands. Pick up & loop the last two diagonal yellow bands to the centre pin.

Step 12

Refer to Steps 5-9 on page 33 & all of page 34 to finish the bracelet with a green extension & C-clip

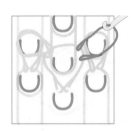

COLOUR IDEAS

Try other colour combinations. Substitue blue for the green & aqua for the yellow or white for the green & pink for the yellow. For the rainbow bracelet, start with the yellow bands; then add pink, red, purple, blue, aqua & green bands.

BUTTERFLY BLOSSOMS
LEVEL: Expert

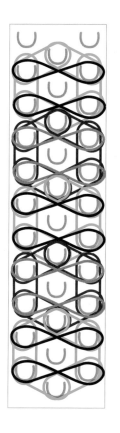

Place the
first pink band

Place the
second pink band

Step 3

Place the third
pink band

Step 4

Place the fourth
pink band

Step 5

Place the fifth
pink band

Step 6

Place the sixth pink band
completing the hexagon

Step 7

Twist a white band into a
figure 8 & place it on the pins

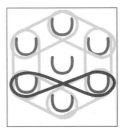

Step 8

Twist another white band
& place it on the pins

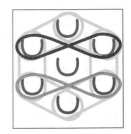

Step 9

Repeat with six aqua bands & two purple bands. Continue to
place the pink, white, aqua & purple bands on the pins until you
reach the top of the loom (see the Chart on page 21).

Step 1

Place a doubled white band on the centre pin

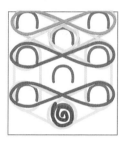

Step 2

Grab the top aqua band on the centre pin

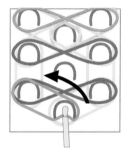

Step 3

Loop the band to the left pin

Step 4

Grab the next aqua band on the centre pin

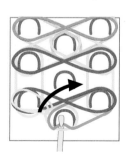

Step 5

Loop the band to the right pin

Step 6

Grab the bottom aqua band on the left pin

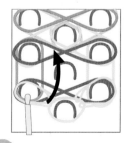

Step 7

Loop the band straight up to the next pin

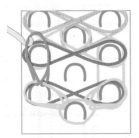

Step 8

Grab the bottom aqua band on the right pin

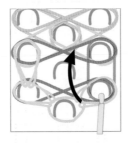

Step 9

Loop the band straight up to the next pin

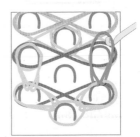

Step 10

Grab the bottom aqua band on the left pin

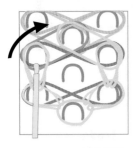

Step 11

Loop the band to the centre pin

Step 12

Grab the bottom aqua band on the right pin

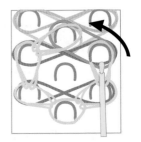

Step 13

Loop the band to the centre pin

Step 14

Continue picking up & looping the pink & aqua bands until you've looped the last blossom.

Step 15

Refer to Steps 5-9 on page 33 & all of page 34 to finish the bracelet with a white extension & C-clip

CHAIN MAIL
LEVEL: Expert

NOTE: When placing the bands:
• Place the loom on the table with the open parts of the pins facing right • Use your fingers to place the bands on the loom
• Follow the steps when placing the bands • Push each band down after you place it on the pins.

Step 1

Twist brown bands into figure 8's & place on pins 1-4

Step 2

Twist and orange band into a figure 8 & place it on pins 2 & 3

> **NOTE:** When Looping the bands:
> • Always use the looping tool to pick up & loop the bands

Step 1

Grab the brown
band on pin 2

Step 2

Loop the brown band
to the front of pin 2

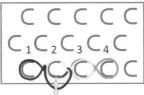

Step 3

Grab the brown
band on pin 3

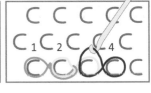

Step 4

Loop the brown band
to the front of pin 3

Step 5

Place 2 more brown
bands on pins 1-4

Step 6

Grab the brown
band on pin 1

Step 7

Loop the brown
band to the front of pin 1

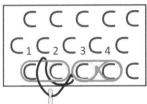

Step 8

Grab the orange
band on pin 2

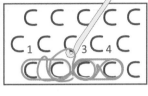

Step 9

Loop the orange band to
the front of pin 2

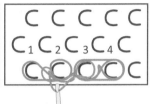

Step 10

Grab the orange
band on pin 3

Step 11

Loop the orange band
to the front of pin 3

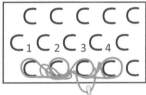

Step 12

Grab the brown
band on pin 4

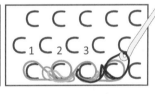

Step 13

Loop the brown band
to the front of pin 4

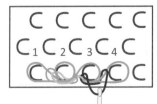

Step 14

Place an orange
band on pins 2 & 3

Step 15

Grab the brown
band on pin 2

Step 16

Loop the brown band to the front of pin 2

Step 17

Grab the brown band on pin 3

Step 18

Loop the brown band to the front of pin 3

Step 19

Continue adding & looping the bands

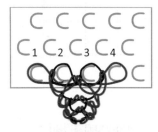

Step 19

Beginning with Step 5, continue adding & looping brown & orange bands. The bracelet will extend from the pins.

Step 20

When the bracelet is long enough, loop the brown band on pin 1 to pin 2 & loop the brown band on pin 4 to pin 3.

Step 21

Refer to steps 5-8 on page 33 & step 5 on page 34 to join the bracelet ends with a C-clip.

TIPS

The Chain Mail bracelet looks great in all sorts of colour combinations; try red & white or dark green & lime green. Our red & black bracelet is made on 6 pins instead of 4- what an easy way to made a wider cuff!

ZIPPY CHAIN
LEVEL: Medium

Step 1

Place the
first red band

Step 2

Place a
white band

Step 3

Place the second
red band

Step 4

Place the first
blue band

Step 5

Place the second
blue band

Step 6

Place 2
red bands

Step 7

Place a
white band

Step 8

Moving up the loom &
starting from Step 4,
continue to place blue,
red & white bands on the
loom pins until you reach
the top of the loom (see
the Chart on page 29).
Place a white band in a
triangle over the last 3
pins.

COLOUR IDEAS

For our aqua, black & blue combo, substitute aqua for the blue, black for
the white & blue for the red; for the white, gold & dark brown combo,
substitute white for the blue, gold for the white & dark brown for the
red. Or make one in camo colours using brown for the blue, black for the
white & green for the red

Looping

Step 1

Grab the top blue band on the centre pin

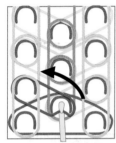

Step 2

Loop the blue band to the left pin

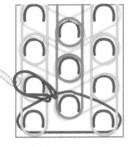

Step 3

Grab the remaining blue band on the centre pin

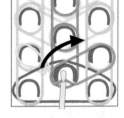

Step 4

Loop the blue band to the right pin

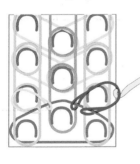

Step 5

Grab the white band on the centre pin

Step 6

Loop the white band straight up to the next pin

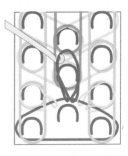

Step 7

Continue picking up & looping the blue & white bands until you've looped the last white band.

Step 9

Grab the red band on the left pin

Step 10

Loop the red band straight up to the next pin

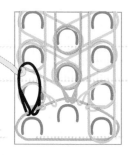

Step 8

Go back to the bottom of the loom & follow steps 9-12 to pick up & loop the red bands until you've looped the last set of vertical red bands. Pick up & loop the last 2 diagonal red bands to the centre pin.

Step 11

Grab the red band on the right pin

Step 12

Loop the red band straight up to the next pin

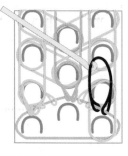

Step 13

Refer to Steps 5-9 on page 33 & all of page 34 to finish the bracelet with a blue extension & C-clip.

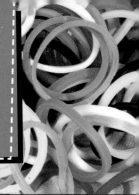

Making a
BRACELET EXTENSION

Many bracelets need an extension to be long enough to wear; the project instructions will tell when to make one. The extension is also made on the loom pins. Follow steps 1-9 to remove the bracelet from the loom.

Step 1

Grab the loops on the left pin

Step 2

Move the loops to the centre pin

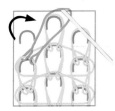

Step 3

Grab the loops on the right pin

Step 4

Move the loops to the centre pin

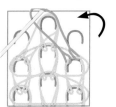

Step 5

Grab all the loops on the centre pin

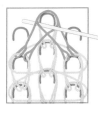

Step 6

Pull a new band halfway through the loops

Step 7

Slide the looping tool through the opposite end of the new band

Step 8

Position the loops on the indented section of the looping tool

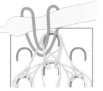

Step 9

Carefully remove the bracelet from the pins & set aside

NOTE: When placing the bands: • Turn the loom so the open parts of the pins facing away from you • Starting at the loom bottom, use your fingers to place the bands on the loom (refer to your project instructions for band colour & see the chart on the left • Push each band down after you place it on the pins

NOTE: When looping the bands: • Turn the loom around so the open parts of the pins are facing you • Always use the looping tool to pick up & loop the bands.

Step 1

Transfer the bands on the looping tool to the bottom pin

Step 2

Grab the first extension band

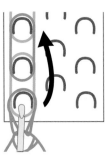

Step 3

Loop the band straight up to the next pin

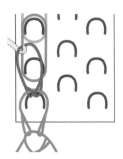

Step 4

Continue picking up & looping the extension bands until you've looped the last band.

Step 5

Slide a C-clip on the band loops

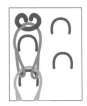

Step 6

Pull the band with the C-clip off the pin. Carefully pull all the bands from the pins. Join the bracelet by slipping the C-clip through the loop (or loops) at the other end of the bracelet